Giving Thanks

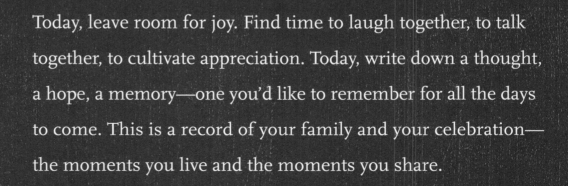

Today, leave room for joy. Find time to laugh together, to talk together, to cultivate appreciation. Today, write down a thought, a hope, a memory—one you'd like to remember for all the days to come. This is a record of your family and your celebration— the moments you live and the moments you share.

What are you
most grateful for?

What will you remember
about this year?

What's worth
celebrating right now?

Who adds joy
to your life ?

What are you
most grateful for?

What will you remember
about this year?

What's worth
celebrating right now?

Who adds joy
to your life ?

What are you
most grateful for?

What will you remember
about this year?

What's worth
celebrating right now?

Who adds joy
to your life ?

What are you
most grateful for?

What will you remember
about this year?

What's worth
celebrating right now?

Who adds joy
to your life ?

Today

is a day to join together.

Today is a day to celebrate. Today, we gather around a table that is bright with shared memories and touched by countless blessings. We are reminded of the year we've had: a year filled with gifts and moments we will take with us, times we will cherish. It is a day to delight in all we have been given.

What are you
most grateful for?

What will you remember
about this year?

What's worth
celebrating right now?

Who adds joy
to your life ?

What are you
most grateful for?

What will you remember
about this year?

What's worth
celebrating right now?

Who adds joy
to your life ?

What are you
most grateful for?

What will you remember
about this year?

What's worth
celebrating right now?

Who adds joy
to your life ?

What are you
most grateful for?

What will you remember
about this year?

What's worth
celebrating right now?

Who adds joy
to your life ?

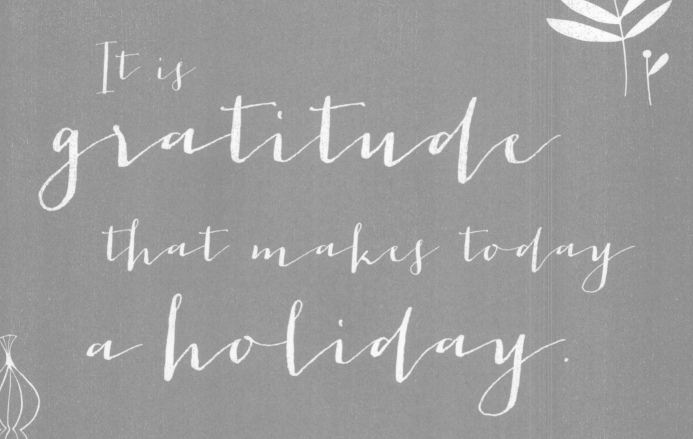

It is *gratitude* that makes today a *holiday*.

Gratitude is what warms us, what brings us together, and what sustains us, too. It is the reason we are here; it is what we have looked forward to. This year, let's bring the spirit of this day into all the days that follow and fill even everyday moments with a sense of true thanksgiving.

What are you
most grateful for?

What will you remember
about this year?

What's worth
celebrating right now?

Who adds joy
to your life ?

What are you
most grateful for?

What will you remember
about this year?

What's worth
celebrating right now?

Who adds joy
to your life ?

What are you
most grateful for?

What will you remember
about this year?

What's worth
celebrating right now?

Who adds joy
to your life ?

What are you
most grateful for?

What will you remember
about this year?

What's worth
celebrating right now?

Who adds joy
to your life ?

We bring so much to this table today.

We bring hearts full of hopes and challenges, joys and concerns. We bring our complicated lives—our losses, our loves, our dreams come true. We bring ourselves, whole and complete, and the relationships that we share. We are linked, we are joined, we are held together by love—and for this we are grateful.

What are you
most grateful for?

What will you remember
about this year?

What's worth
celebrating right now?

Who adds joy
to your life ?

What are you
most grateful for?

What will you remember
about this year?

What's worth
celebrating right now?

Who adds joy
to your life ?

What are you
most grateful for?

What will you remember
about this year?

What's worth
celebrating right now?

Who adds joy
to your life?

What are you
most grateful for?

What will you remember
about this year?

What's worth
celebrating right now?

Who adds joy
to your life ?

Today, we
give thanks for the
memories
we share
and the ways they
bring us closer.

We celebrate the bright times that lift our spirits and
fill us up. We honor the hard times that give us a chance
to support each other. And we give thanks for the
memories we are making today—we will keep them,
we will hold them in our hearts.

What are you
most grateful for?

What will you remember
about this year?

What's worth
celebrating right now?

Who adds joy
to your life ?

What are you
most grateful for?

What will you remember
about this year?

What's worth
celebrating right now?

Who adds joy
to your life ?

What are you
most grateful for?

What will you remember
about this year?

What's worth
celebrating right now?

Who adds joy
to your life ?

What are you
most grateful for?

What will you remember
about this year?

What's worth
celebrating right now?

Who adds joy
to your life ?

Today, we
give thanks for
small
pleasures
and simple
blessings.

For good food, for laughter, for time well spent. For moments of delight, for family roots, for honored traditions. In this one day, we have been given so many of life's greatest gifts. We are blessed to live in such abundance—and blessed again to share in it together.

What are you
most grateful for?

What will you remember
about this year?

What's worth
celebrating right now?

Who adds joy
to your life ?

What are you
most grateful for?

What will you remember
about this year?

What's worth
celebrating right now?

Who adds joy
to your life ?

What are you
most grateful for?

What will you remember
about this year?

What's worth
celebrating right now?

Who adds joy
to your life ?

What are you
most grateful for?

What will you remember
about this year?

What's worth
celebrating right now?

Who adds joy
to your life ?

This year
has been like
so many
of the years
that have gone
before~

filled with times of love, times of connection, times of
celebration. But this year has also been a new year—
filled with change, with growth, with the unexpected.
We gather today in a spirit of gratitude that we are here,
right now, sharing our lives, supporting each other,
making these moments count.

What are you
most grateful for?

What will you remember
about this year?

What's worth
celebrating right now?

Who adds joy
to your life ?

What are you
most grateful for?

What will you remember
about this year?

What's worth
celebrating right now?

Who adds joy
to your life ?

What are you
most grateful for?

What will you remember
about this year?

What's worth
celebrating right now?

Who adds joy
to your life ?

What are you
most grateful for?

What will you remember
about this year?

What's worth
celebrating right now?

Who adds joy
to your life ?

The best thing
we can do with our
gratitude
is experience it and
express it—to show our
appreciation
for both the giver
and the gift.

We can express our thanks through quiet moments or with bold gestures. We can express it with words or in actions, in small ripples or great big waves. Today is a day to feel and to share, to show our appreciation for the people and the gifts that make our world everything it is.

What are you
most grateful for?

What will you remember
about this year?

What's worth
celebrating right now?

Who adds joy
to your life ?

What are you
most grateful for?

What will you remember
about this year?

What's worth
celebrating right now?

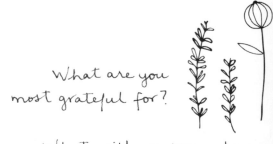

Who adds joy
to your life ?

What are you
most grateful for?

What will you remember
about this year?

What's worth
celebrating right now?

Who adds joy
to your life ?

Thanksgiving is a holiday of the heart.

It is a day to celebrate of all the priceless things that we feel and experience together. Today, we celebrate connection, we cherish laughter, we treasure silliness and seriousness and joy so big it spills over. We are filled with gratitude for the warmth between us, the ways we're joined, and all the good things we share.

COMPENDIUM.

live inspired

WITH SPECIAL THANKS TO THE
ENTIRE COMPENDIUM FAMILY.

CREDITS:

Written by: M.H. Clark
Designed by: Heidi Rodriguez
Edited by: Amelia Riedler
Creative Direction by: Julie Flahiff